Name : ___________________

Subtraction Worksheets

17 − 15	8 − 2	5 − 3

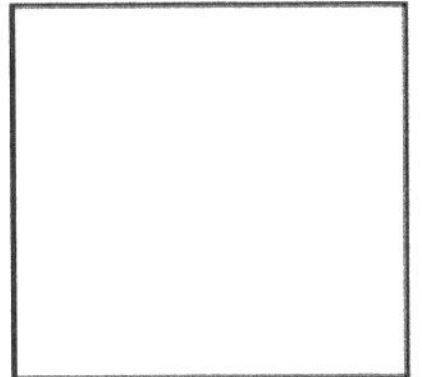
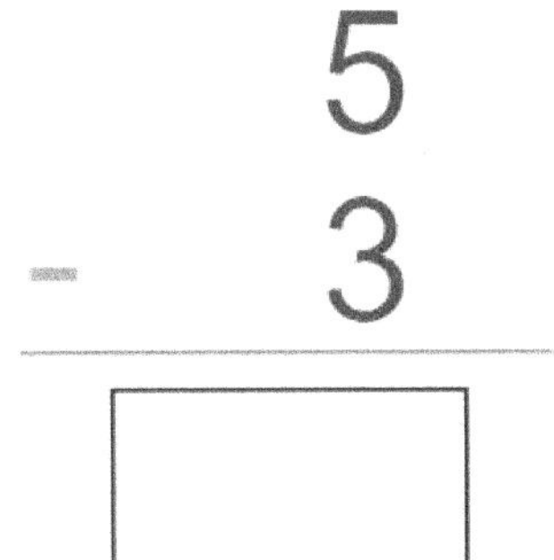

7 − 6	13 − 2	11 − 4

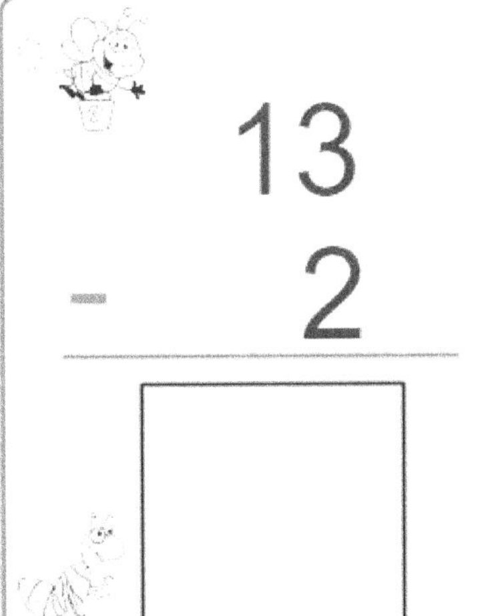
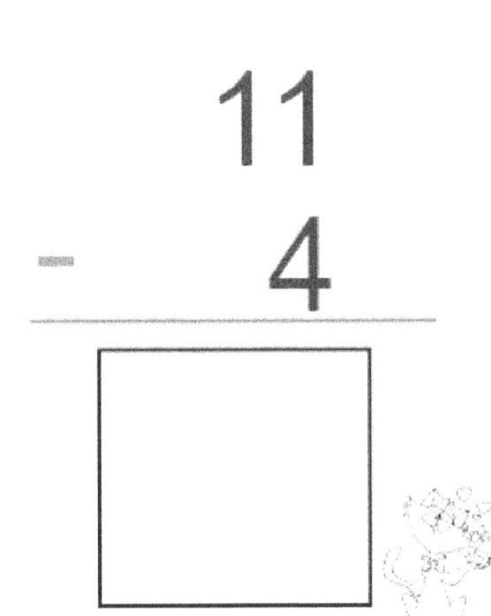

1 − 1	8 − 5	11 − 4

Math Made Easy....

Name : _______________________

Direction: Use the picture to help you find the answer.

1 2 3 4 5 6 7 8 9 10

12 - 11 = ____

6 - 2 = ____

14 - 3 = ____

9 - 1 = ____

13 - 11 = ____

19 - 16 = ____

16 - 4 = ____

11 - 5 = ____

12 - 9 = ____

7 - 4 = ____

Name : ______________

Subtraction Worksheets

	19
−	9

	3
−	2

	18
−	1

	12
−	11

	10
−	2

	8
−	1

	7
−	2

	3
−	1

	9
−	3

Math Made Easy....

Name : _______________________________

Direction: Use the picture to help you find the answer.

| 1 | 2 | 3 | 4 | 5 | 6 | 7 | 8 | 9 | 10 |

4 - 1 = ____

4 - 2 = ____

7 - 6 = ____

16 - 6 = ____

5 - 2 = ____

18 - 12 = ____

13 - 6 = ____

13 - 9 = ____

20 - 12 = ____

4 - 2 = ____

Subtraction Worksheets

13 − 4	14 − 10	4 − 1
16 − 4	4 − 3	17 − 5
17 − 6	2 − 1	13 − 2

Math Made Easy....

Name : _______________________________

Direction: Use the picture to help you find the answer.

| 1 | 2 | 3 | 4 | 5 | 6 | 7 | 8 | 9 | 10 |

$1 - 1 =$

$5 - 4 =$

$15 - 3 =$

$3 - 2 =$

$14 - 4 =$

$17 - 14 =$

$7 - 5 =$

$19 - 3 =$

$14 - 8 =$

$15 - 11 =$

Subtraction Worksheets

Name : _______________

7 − 4	1 − 1	5 − 1
5 − 4	1 − 1	7 − 4
15 − 14	12 − 7	8 − 6

Math Made Easy....

Name : _______________________

Direction: Use the picture to help you find the answer. 

1 2 3 4 5 6 7 8 9 10

2 - 1 = ___

7 - 5 = ___

14 - 8 = ___

7 - 2 = ___

8 - 7 = ___

13 - 4 = ___

19 - 9 = ___

13 - 8 = ___

16 - 11 = ___

14 - 13 = ___

Subtraction Worksheets

| 8 | 18 | 7 |
| 3 | 1 | 6 |

| 12 | 20 | 8 |
| 6 | 13 | 2 |

| 11 | 20 | 12 |
| 1 | 17 | 8 |

Math Made Easy....

20 - 3 ___	14 - 5 ___
8 - 4 ___	9 - 8 ___
7 - 1 ___	8 - 6 ___
7 - 4 ___	19 - 15 ___
8 - 7 ___	2 - 1 ___

Subtraction Worksheets

3 - 1	17 - 14	9 - 5
10 - 9	5 - 4	16 - 12
16 - 4	11 - 7	15 - 4

3 - 2 =

2 - 1 =

2 - 1 =

8 - 7 =

18 - 6 =

15 - 6 =

13 - 12 =

12 - 7 =

20 - 10 =

13 - 12 =

Subtraction Worksheets

	19		16		7
−	7	−	10	−	2

	13		11		18
−	2	−	7	−	4

	15		19		3
−	7	−	4	−	1

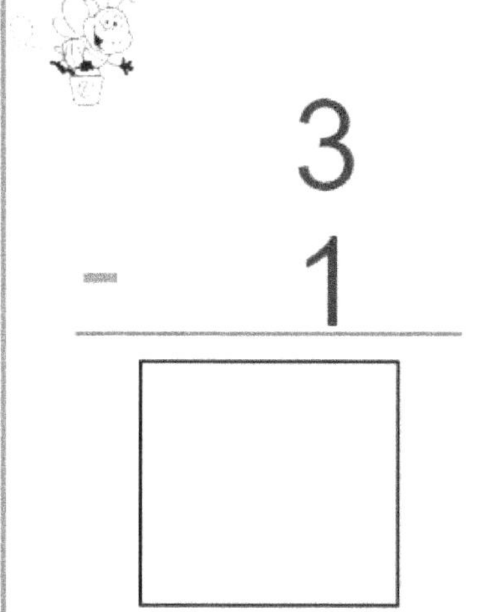

Math Made Easy....

Name : _______________________________

Direction: Use the picture to help you find the answer.

1   2   3   4   5   6   7   8   9   10

18 - 6 ___	2 - 1 ___
9 - 5 ___	1 - 1 ___
11 - 9 ___	12 - 3 ___
18 - 15 ___	13 - 9 ___
14 - 9 ___	16 - 11 ___

Subtraction Worksheets

14 − 11 ☐	8 − 5 ☐	16 − 12 ☐
16 − 14 ☐	20 − 8 ☐	14 − 10 ☐
6 − 3 ☐	11 − 2 ☐	1 − 1 ☐

Name : _______________________________

Direction: Use the picture to help you find the answer.

2 - 1 __	10 - 5 __
12 - 8 __	14 - 2 __
19 - 12 __	11 - 8 __
20 - 17 __	19 - 10 __
18 - 11 __	7 - 6 __

16 − 2	20 − 13	10 − 9
8 − 3	20 − 17	5 − 4
17 − 14	19 − 7	7 − 3

Name : _______________________________

Direction: Use the picture to help you find the answer.

| 1 | 2 | 3 | 4 | 5 | 6 | 7 | 8 | 9 | 10 |

$5 - 2 = $ ___

$3 - 2 = $ ___

$2 - 1 = $ ___

$7 - 5 = $ ___

$18 - 7 = $ ___

$15 - 12 = $ ___

$18 - 7 = $ ___

$17 - 16 = $ ___

$10 - 8 = $ ___

$9 - 1 = $ ___

Subtraction Worksheets

14 − 5	2 − 1	10 − 7
9 − 4	3 − 1	1 − 1
17 − 6	20 − 2	15 − 1

Name : ___________________________

Direction: Use the picture to help you find the answer.

| 1 | 2 | 3 | 4 | 5 | 6 | 7 | 8 | 9 | 10 |

15 - 4 = ___

4 - 2 = ___

7 - 1 = ___

11 - 9 = ___

12 - 2 = ___

2 - 1 = ___

13 - 1 = ___

13 - 12 = ___

1 - 1 = ___

18 - 14 = ___

17 − 2 =	8 − 3 =	16 − 8 =
14 − 12 =	14 − 12 =	19 − 7 =
2 − 1 =	5 − 4 =	3 − 2 =

Name : _______________________________

Direction: Use the picture to help you find the answer.

| 1 | 2 | 3 | 4 | 5 | 6 | 7 | 8 | 9 | 10 |

20 - 13 = _______

13 - 3 = _______

9 - 5 = _______

11 - 4 = _______

15 - 9 = _______

5 - 2 = _______

10 - 6 = _______

3 - 2 = _______

8 - 3 = _______

3 - 1 = _______

Subtraction Worksheets

20 − 11	2 − 1	20 − 12
14 − 9	18 − 13	16 − 8
8 − 3	18 − 12	2 − 1

Direction: Use the picture to help you find the answer.

18 - 13 __	6 - 4 __
8 - 3 __	4 - 1 __
16 - 15 __	20 - 14 __
10 - 6 __	15 - 5 __
20 - 15 __	14 - 4 __

Subtraction Worksheets

2 − 1	12 − 6	16 − 8
18 − 10	17 − 4	19 − 2
2 − 1	10 − 4	11 − 5

Math Made Easy....

Name : _______________________

Direction: Use the picture to help you find the answer.

1   2   3   4   5   6   7   8   9   10

$2 - 1 = $ _______

$10 - 9 = $ _______

$15 - 6 = $ _______

$6 - 1 = $ _______

$15 - 11 = $ _______

$13 - 12 = $ _______

$7 - 4 = $ _______

$15 - 12 = $ _______

$7 - 4 = $ _______

$3 - 2 = $ _______

Subtraction Worksheets

	3		6		6
−	1	−	5	−	3

	19		7		19
−	3	−	4	−	2

	10		12		11
−	5	−	3	−	8

Math Made Easy....

Name : _______________________________

Direction: Use the picture to help you find the answer. 

16 - 12 = ___

14 - 1 = ___

18 - 11 = ___

9 - 8 = ___

20 - 2 = ___

14 - 6 = ___

4 - 1 = ___

17 - 4 = ___

19 - 4 = ___

6 - 1 = ___

Subtraction Worksheets

15	7	10
− 8	− 5	− 8

18	12	4
− 16	− 4	− 2

12	9	2
− 2	− 6	− 1

Math Made Easy....

Name : _______________________________

Direction: Use the picture to help you find the answer.

1	2	3	4	5	6	7	8	9	10

14 - 9 = ______

5 - 1 = ______

3 - 2 = ______

8 - 3 = ______

4 - 3 = ______

1 - 1 = ______

16 - 3 = ______

16 - 8 = ______

7 - 6 = ______

18 - 3 = ______

Name :

Subtraction Worksheets

	10
−	6

	7
−	3

	1
−	1

	20
−	14

	16
−	2

	5
−	2

	3
−	1

	3
−	1

	16
−	8

Math Made Easy....

Name : ___________________________________

Direction: Use the picture to help you find the answer.

| 1 | 2 | 3 | 4 | 5 | 6 | 7 | 8 | 9 | 10 |

9 - 1 = ____

9 - 7 = ____

16 - 7 = ____

5 - 4 = ____

5 - 1 = ____

13 - 12 = ____

7 - 4 = ____

13 - 6 = ____

11 - 7 = ____

13 - 4 = ____

Subtraction Worksheets

14 − 11	11 − 4	18 − 15
17 − 9	15 − 6	9 − 2
10 − 6	3 − 2	3 − 1

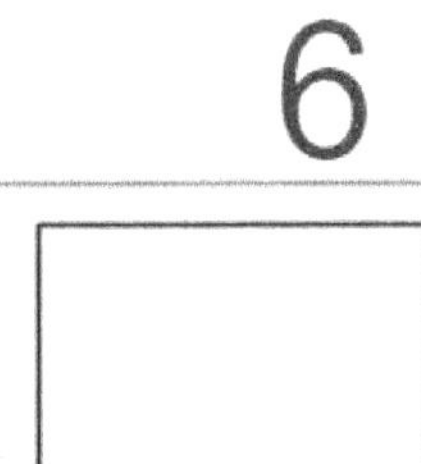

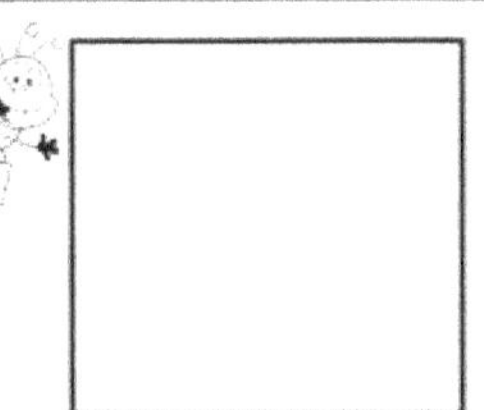

Math Made Easy....

13 - 9 =

18 - 10 =

17 - 11 =

10 - 9 =

18 - 15 =

2 - 1 =

20 - 5 =

17 - 13 =

2 - 1 =

18 - 14 =

Subtraction Worksheets

11		6		19
− 1		− 5		− 17

9		8		19
− 3		− 1		− 15

8		20		5
− 1		− 11		− 4

Math Made Easy....

16 - 9 _____

12 - 6 _____

12 - 4 _____

14 - 7 _____

17 - 14 _____

20 - 7 _____

12 - 3 _____

16 - 9 _____

14 - 6 _____

2 - 1 _____

Name : _______________

Subtraction Worksheets

4 − 3	7 − 4	4 − 1
1 − 1	18 − 12	16 − 6
7 − 6	1 − 1	4 − 3

Math Made Easy....

16 - 5 = _____

17 - 3 = _____

3 - 1 = _____

1 - 1 = _____

8 - 7 = _____

11 - 7 = _____

8 - 1 = _____

17 - 7 = _____

14 - 9 = _____

9 - 6 = _____

Subtraction Worksheets

3 − 2	

3
− 2

7
− 3

3
− 1

13
− 6

15
− 4

1
− 1

15
− 12

20
− 6

16
− 4

Name : _______________________________

Direction: Use the picture to help you find the answer.

| 1 | 2 | 3 | 4 | 5 | 6 | 7 | 8 | 9 | 10 |

17 12 ___

19 18 ___

10 7 ___

12 5 ___

11 9 ___

8 2 ___

4 3 ___

9 3 ___

13 3 ___

8 2 ___

Subtraction Worksheets

	11		20		5
−	4	−	15	−	4

	12		6		20
−	2	−	4	−	5

	6		1		2
−	1	−	1	−	1

Math Made Easy....

Name : ______________________

Direction: Use the picture to help you find the answer.

| 1 | 2 | 3 | 4 | 5 | 6 | 7 | 8 | 9 | 10 |

6 - 2 = _____

3 - 2 = _____

2 - 1 = _____

11 - 6 = _____

12 - 2 = _____

18 - 10 = _____

4 - 2 = _____

1 - 1 = _____

6 - 5 = _____

14 - 1 = _____

Name : _______________

Subtraction Worksheets

4 − 1	16 − 14	13 − 7
10 − 8	6 − 5	8 − 3
8 − 2	9 − 7	11 − 4

Math Made Easy….

Name : _______________________________

Direction: Use the picture to help you find the answer.

| 1 | 2 | 3 | 4 | 5 | 6 | 7 | 8 | 9 | 10 |

17 - 6 =

20 - 14 =

7 - 2 =

11 - 3 =

12 - 10 =

13 - 9 =

18 - 4 =

3 - 2 =

5 - 1 =

10 - 9 =

Subtraction Worksheets

Problem 1:
$$11 - 7 = \boxed{}$$

Problem 2:
$$12 - 5 = \boxed{}$$

Problem 3:
$$20 - 14 = \boxed{}$$

Problem 4:
$$13 - 5 = \boxed{}$$

Problem 5:
$$6 - 2 = \boxed{}$$

Problem 6:
$$10 - 5 = \boxed{}$$

Problem 7:
$$12 - 11 = \boxed{}$$

Problem 8:
$$1 - 1 = \boxed{}$$

Problem 9:
$$12 - 2 = \boxed{}$$

Math Made Easy....

Name : _______________________________

Direction: Use the picture to help you find the answer.

| 1 | 2 | 3 | 4 | 5 | 6 | 7 | 8 | 9 | 10 |

14 - 8 = ____

9 - 5 = ____

8 - 7 = ____

8 - 5 = ____

16 - 5 = ____

1 - 1 = ____

2 - 1 = ____

4 - 2 = ____

5 - 2 = ____

10 - 2 = ____

Subtraction Worksheets

7 − 1	20 − 19	10 − 6
8 − 4	20 − 9	15 − 10
2 − 1	18 − 1	13 − 3

Math Made Easy....

Name : _______________________________

Direction: Use the picture to help you find the answer.

8 - 4 =

1 - 1 =

4 - 1 =

3 - 1 =

19 - 17 =

19 - 4 =

10 - 6 =

20 - 6 =

3 - 2 =

16 - 9 =

Subtraction Worksheets

1	2	5
− 1	− 1	− 4

1	19	6
− 1	− 14	− 5

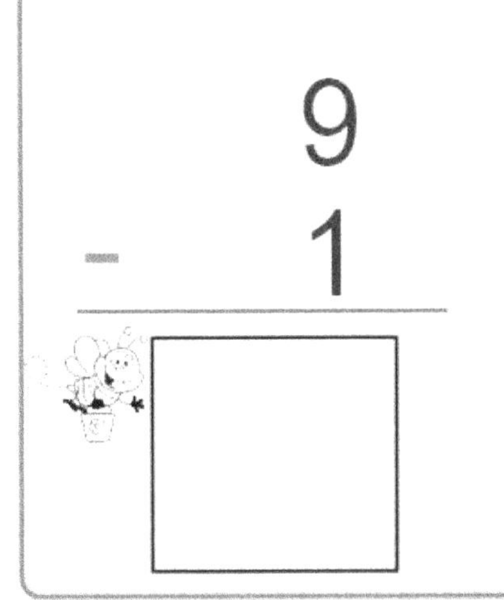

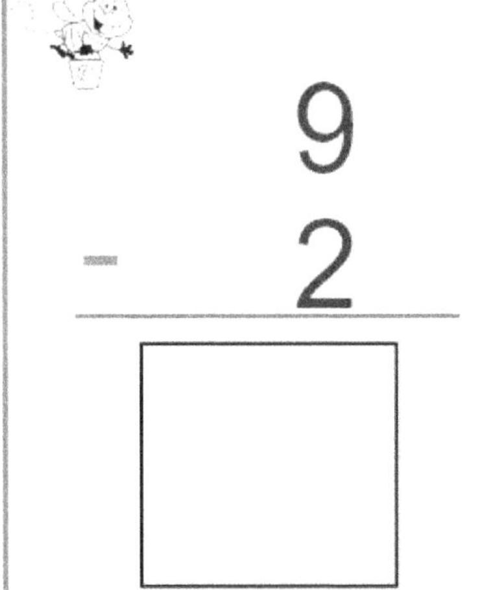

7	9	9
− 5	− 1	− 2

Math Made Easy....

Name : _______________________

Direction: Use the picture to help you find the answer.

1   2   3   4   5   6   7   8   9   10

$1 - 1 =$ $11 - 5 =$

$4 - 3 =$ $8 - 4 =$

$11 - 4 =$ $3 - 1 =$

$10 - 1 =$ $5 - 4 =$

$9 - 8 =$ $17 - 8 =$

Name : _______________

Subtraction Worksheets

6 − 4	8 − 7	10 − 9
6 − 4	2 − 1	14 − 8
6 − 4	6 − 3	1 − 1

Math Made Easy....

Name : _______________________

Addition Worksheets

15	
+ 7	

18	
+ 3	

18	
+ 12	

18	
+ 17	

20	
+ 1	

11	
+ 11	

11	
+ 7	

12	
+ 3	

14	
+ 14	

Math Made Easy....

Addition Worksheets

15 + 7 ▢	18 + 3 ▢	18 + 12 ▢
18 + 17 ▢	20 + 1 ▢	11 + 11 ▢
11 + 7 ▢	12 + 3 ▢	14 + 14 ▢

Direction: Add the number of images in each box and write the answer in the last box.

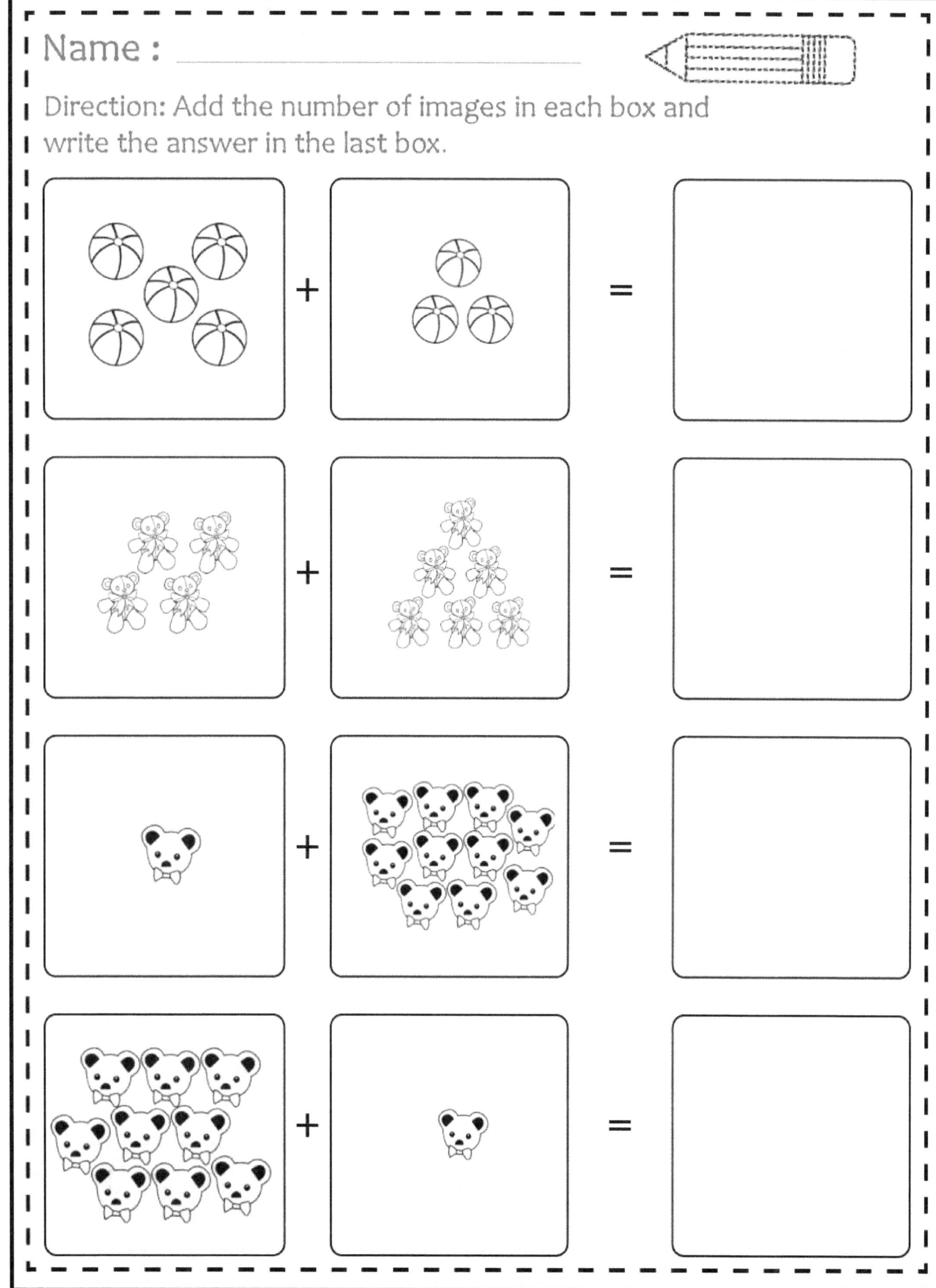

Name : ____________

Addition Worksheets

6
+ 9

Answer

6
+ 1

Answer

4
+ 6

Answer

3
+ 10

Answer

6
+ 7

Answer

1
+ 7

Answer

Addition Worksheets

16 + 19	4 + 6	12 + 3
1 + 13	7 + 15	5 + 6
2 + 10	4 + 11	3 + 16

Name : _______________________

Direction: Add the number of images in each box and
write the answer in the last box.

Addition Worksheets

2 + 5 ——— [ ]　Answer	5 + 9 ——— [ ]　Answer
5 + 8 ——— [ ]　Answer	5 + 6 ——— [ ]　Answer
2 + 7 ——— [ ]　Answer	6 + 4 ——— [ ]　Answer

| | 10 |
| + | 11 |

| | 8 |
| + | 19 |

| | 3 |
| + | 4 |

| | 14 |
| + | 14 |

| | 8 |
| + | 3 |

| | 19 |
| + | 11 |

| | 7 |
| + | 16 |

| | 13 |
| + | 9 |

| | 9 |
| + | 14 |

Direction: Add the number of images in each box and write the answer in the last box.

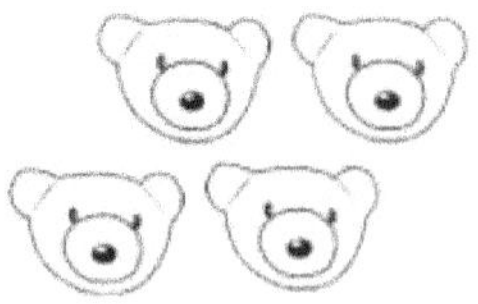

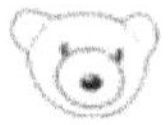

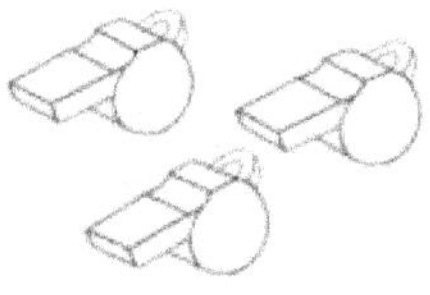

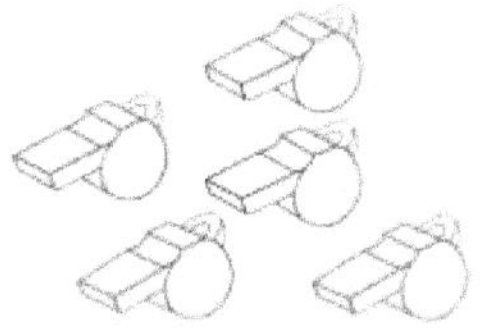

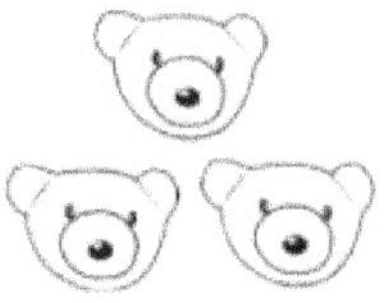

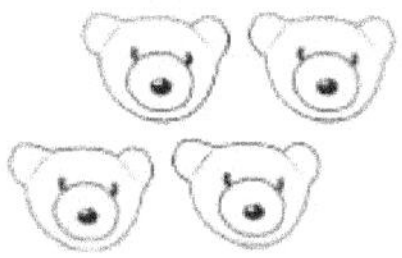

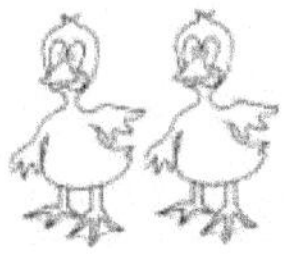

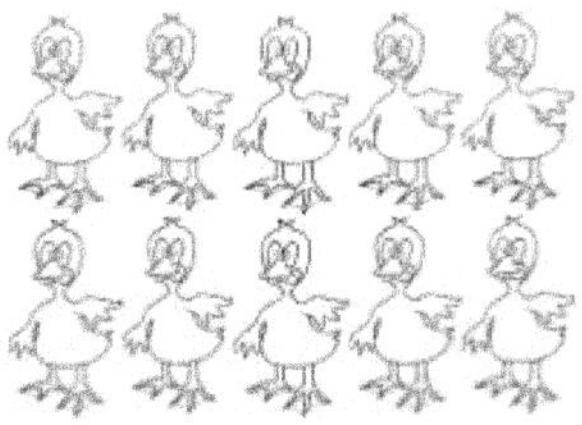

Name : ___________

Addition Worksheets

4

+ 3

Answer

6

+ 2

Answer

5

+ 5

Answer

3

+ 10

Answer

4

+ 8

Answer

4

+ 4

Answer

12 + 18 =	5 + 8 =	18 + 9 =
12 + 14 =	12 + 20 =	20 + 2 =
12 + 20 =	4 + 17 =	14 + 4 =

Name : _______________________

Direction: Add the number of images in each box and
write the answer in the last box.

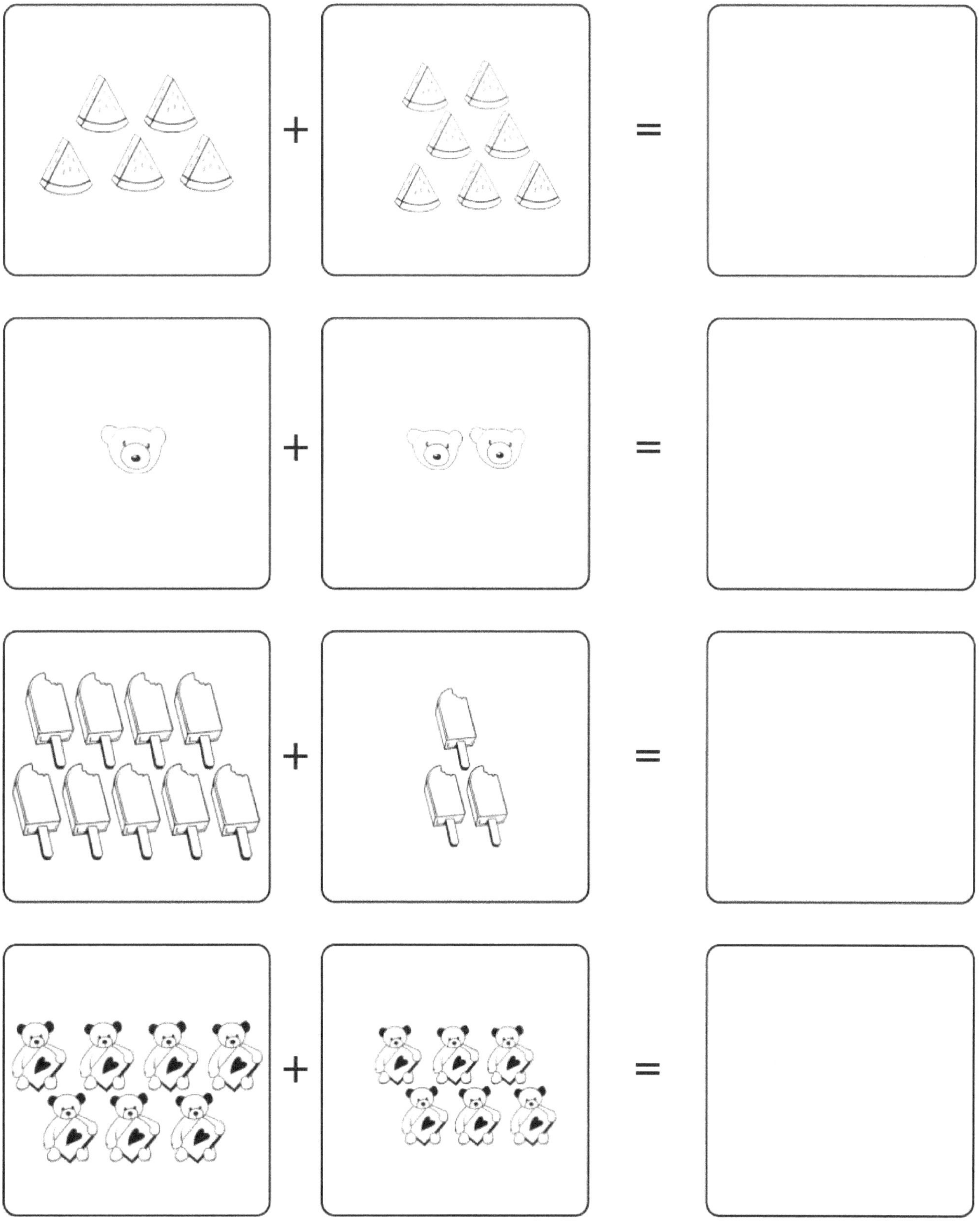

	+	=
	+	=
	+	=
	+	=

Name : _______________

Addition Worksheets

2
+ 10

Answer

4
+ 1

Answer

5
+ 5

Answer

1
+ 9

Answer

4
+ 3

Answer

5
+ 7

Answer

Addition Worksheets

20 + 12	16 + 14	9 + 11
5 + 16	14 + 12	14 + 3
1 + 7	3 + 12	8 + 8

Name : _______________________

Direction: Add the number of images in each box and
write the answer in the last box.

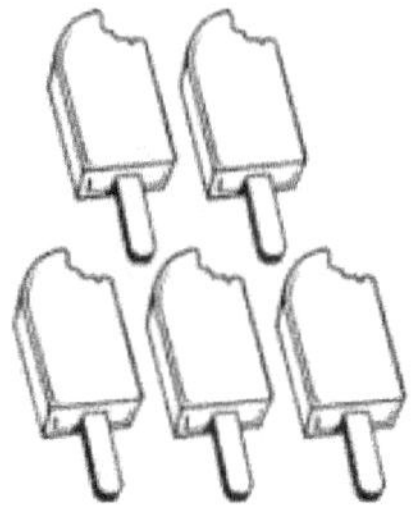

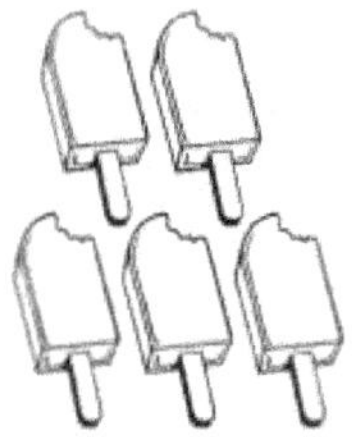

Addition Worksheets

3
+ 6

Answer

3
+ 10

Answer

2
+ 3

Answer

4
+ 2

Answer

1
+ 8

Answer

4
+ 5

Answer

19 + 3	

19
+ 3

19
+ 20

8
+ 19

15
+ 18

17
+ 4

20
+ 4

4
+ 4

14
+ 6

13
+ 6

Direction: Add the number of images in each box and write the answer in the last box.

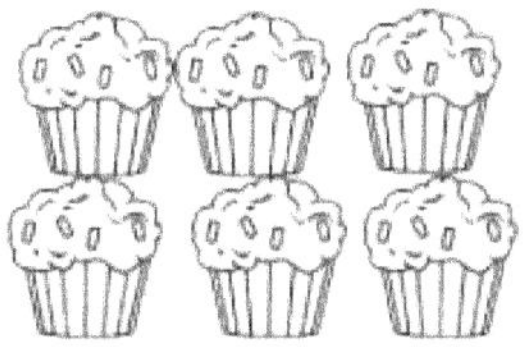

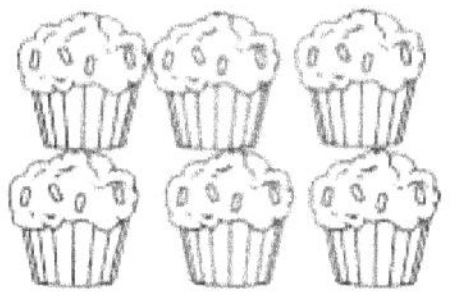

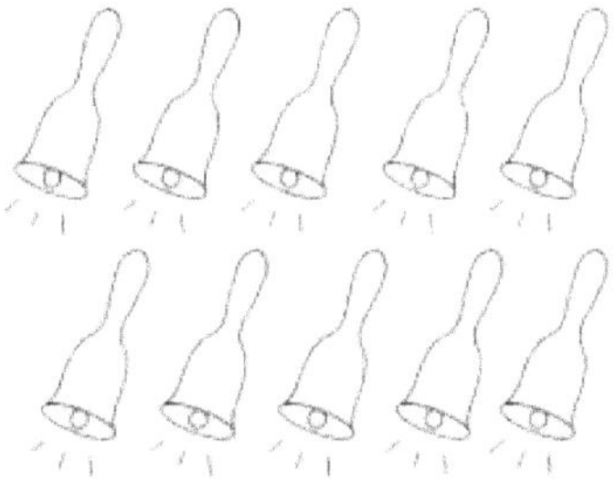

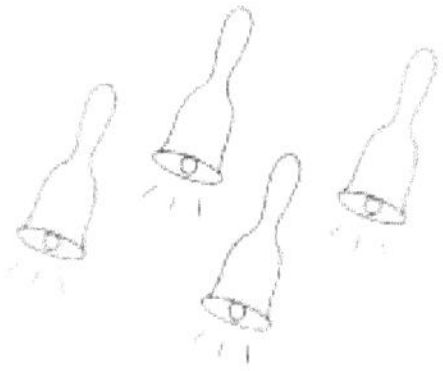

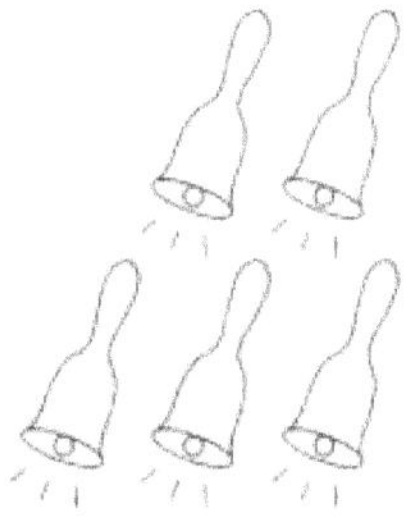

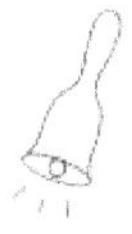

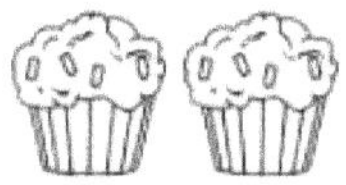

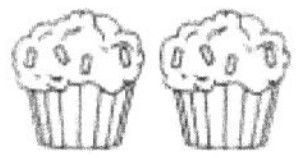

Name : _______________________

Addition Worksheets

1
+ 10

Answer

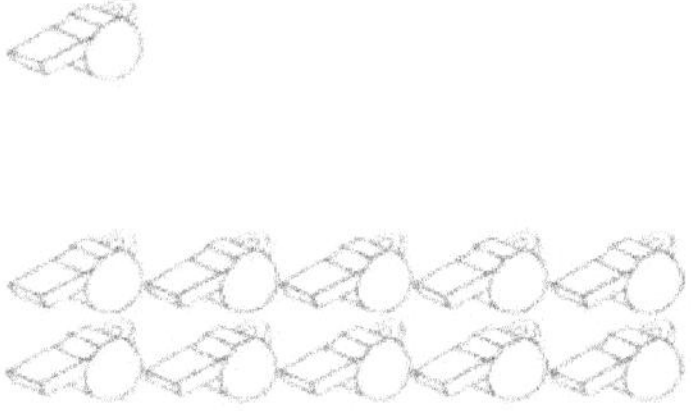

2
+ 10

Answer

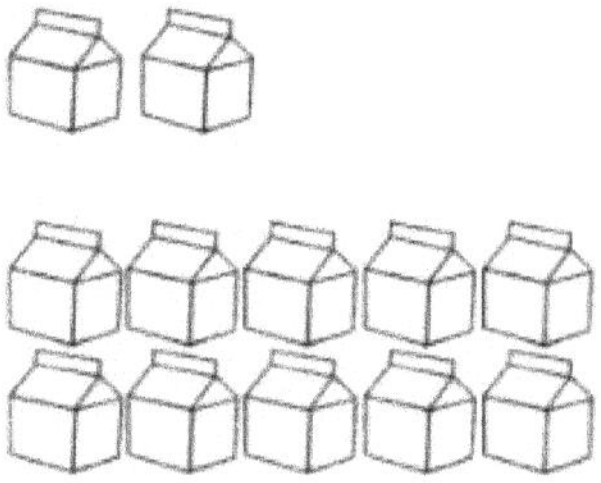

3
+ 10

Answer

2
+ 2

Answer

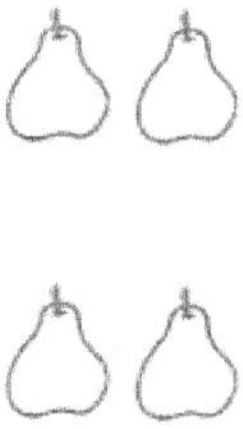

6
+ 8

Answer

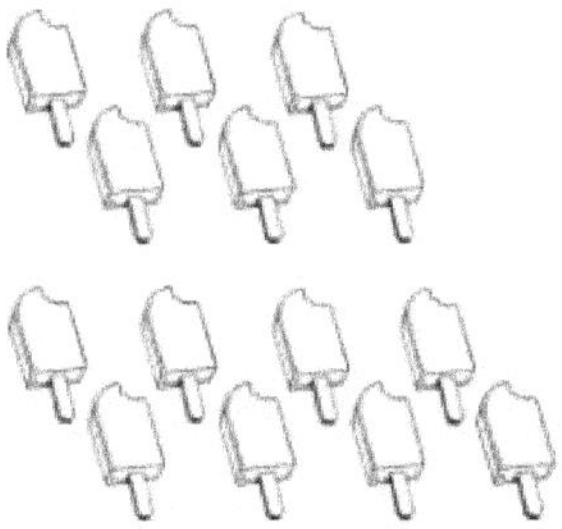

3
+ 10

Answer

Addition Worksheets

16	8	8
+ 5	+ 2	+ 8

7	18	19
+ 18	+ 20	+ 18

15	1	20
+ 18	+ 20	+ 13

Name :
Direction: Add the number of images in each box and
write the answer in the last box.

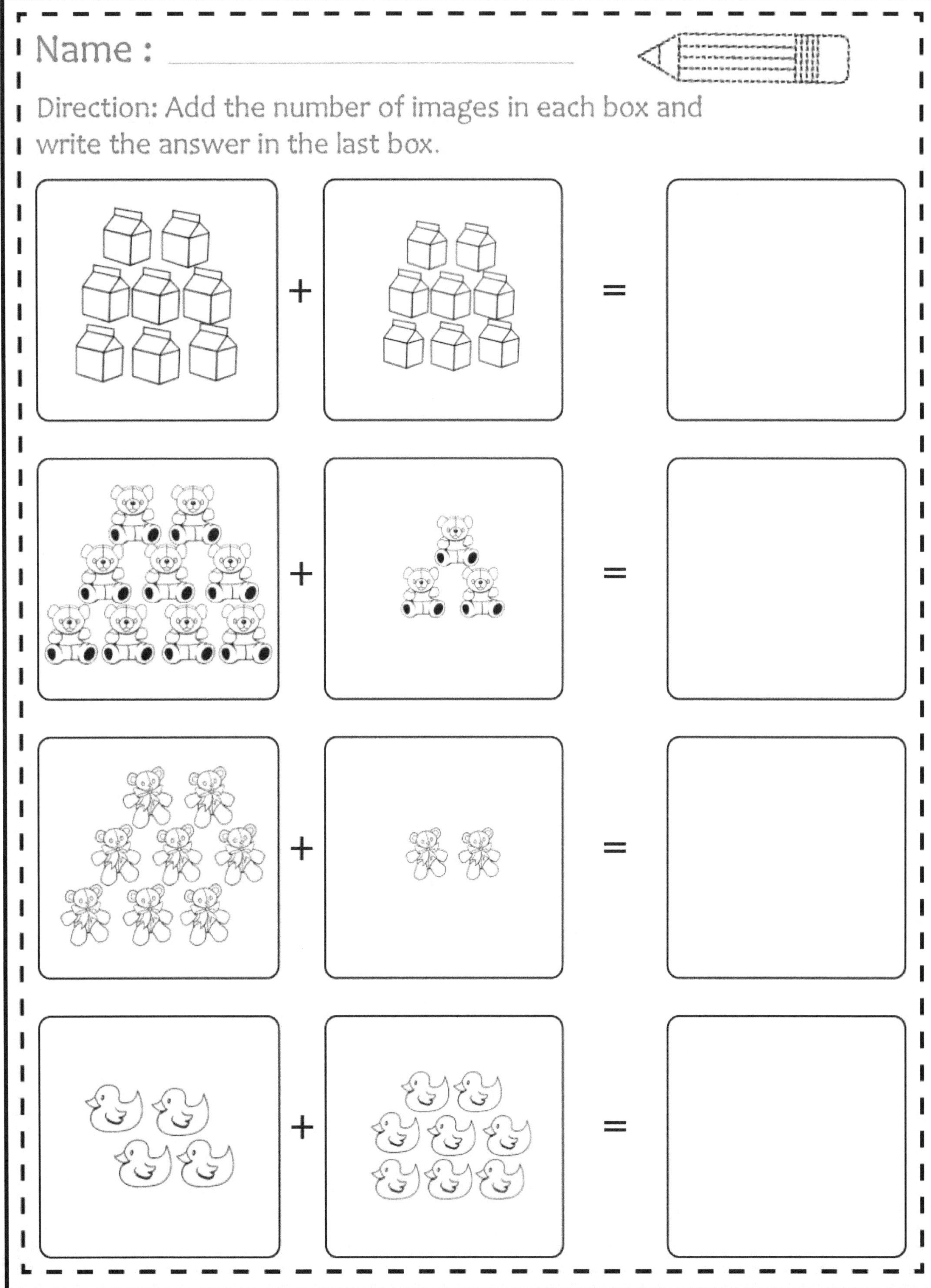

5
+ 8
Answer

5
+ 7
Answer

6
+ 10
Answer

3
+ 10
Answer

5
+ 6
Answer

3
+ 7
Answer

Addition Worksheets

5 + 4	5 + 16	17 + 14
5 + 1	13 + 12	7 + 10
17 + 14	8 + 6	4 + 5

Name : _______________

Direction: Add the number of images in each box and
write the answer in the last box.

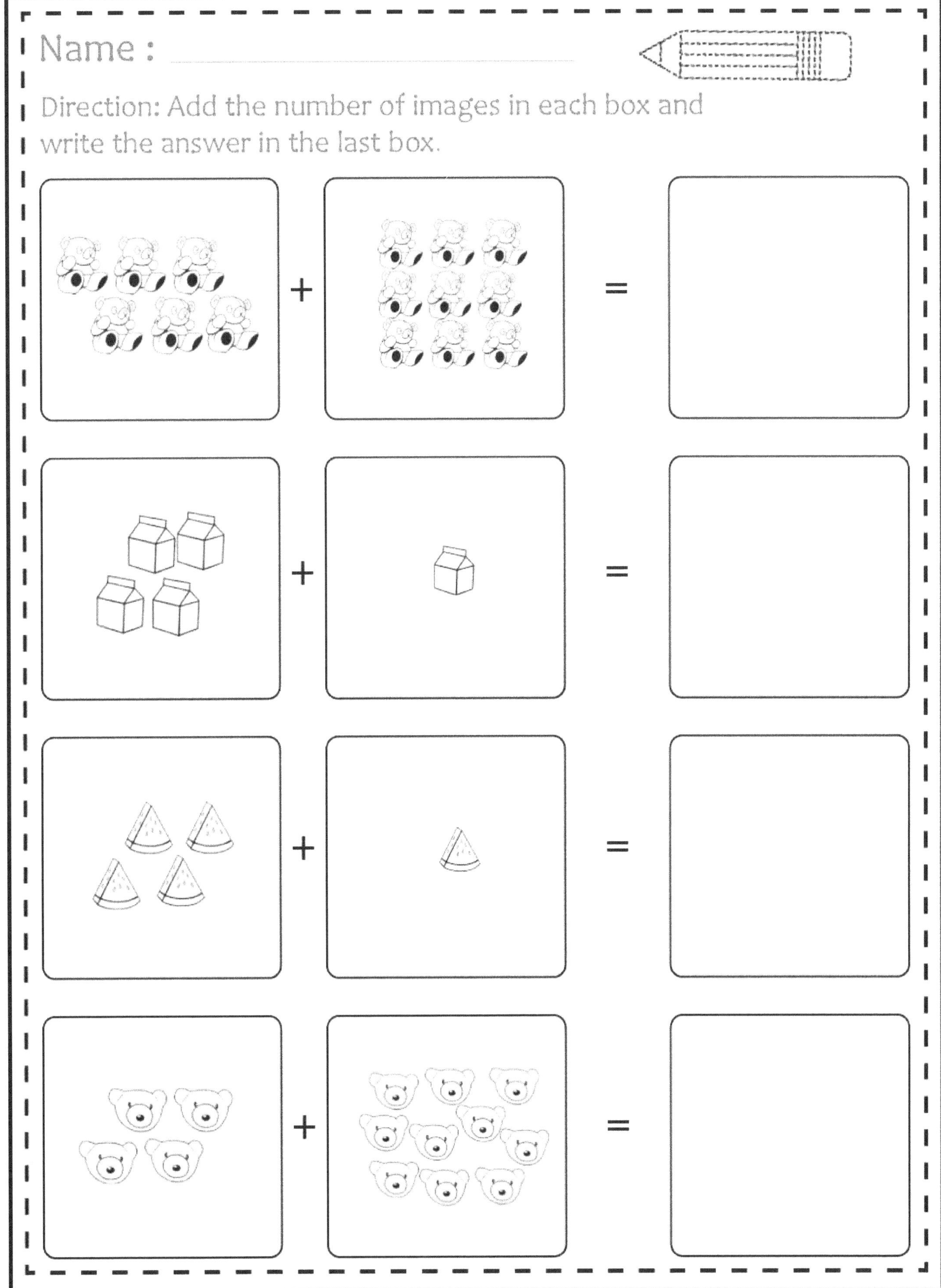

4
+ 6

Answer

5
+ 3

Answer

2
+ 2

Answer

4
+ 5

Answer

4
+ 10

Answer

5
+ 10

Answer

Addition Worksheets

1 + 9	9 + 10	13 + 18
15 + 4	9 + 15	7 + 12
3 + 1	2 + 17	3 + 4

Name : ___________________

Direction: Add the number of images in each box and write the answer in the last box.

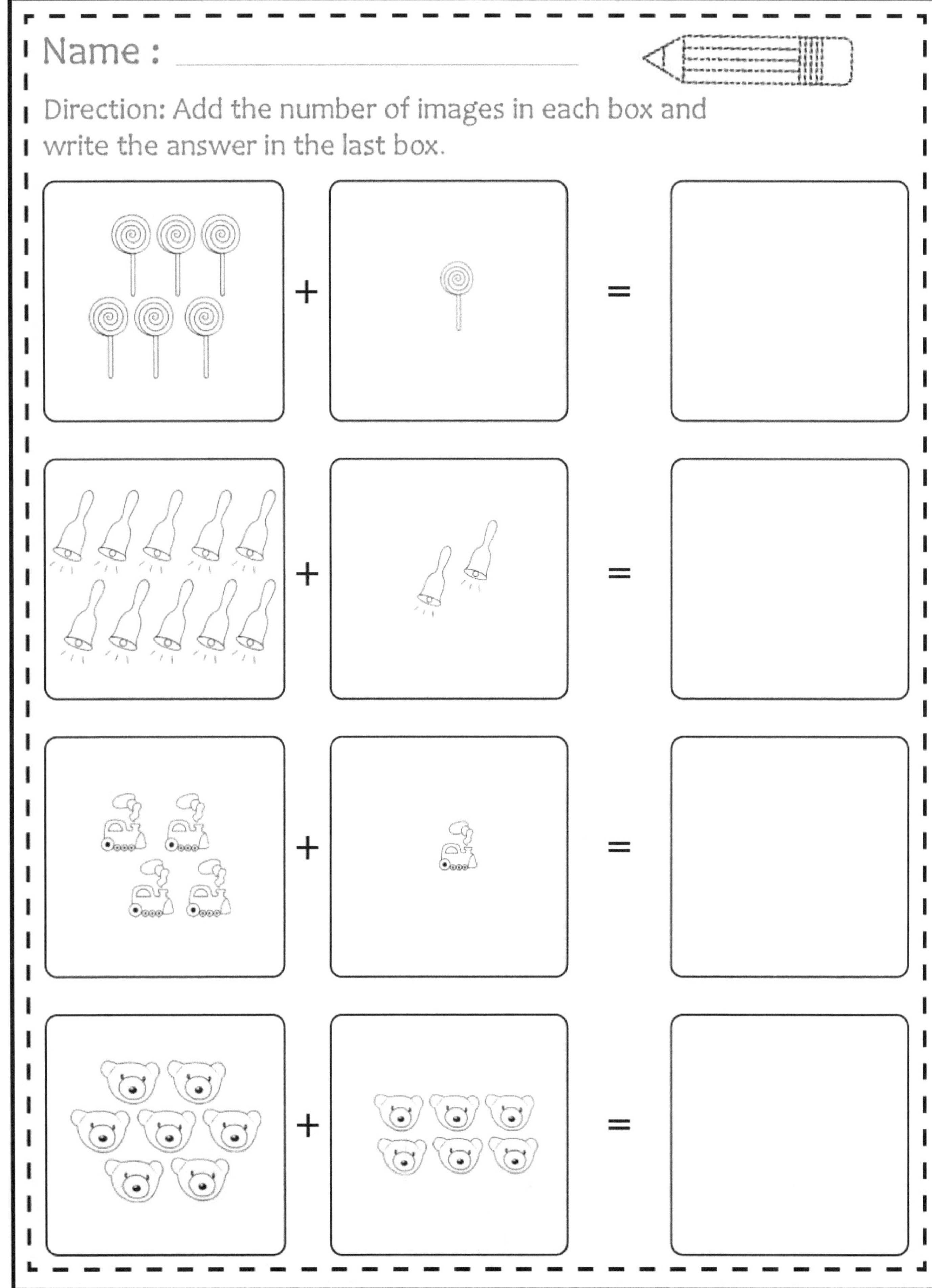

Addition Worksheets

Name: _______________

2
+ 10

Answer

2
+ 6

Answer

6
+ 3

Answer

4
+ 1

Answer

3
+ 6

Answer

3
+ 3

Answer

Addition Worksheets

2 + 14	20 + 8	1 + 9
13 + 2	13 + 1	2 + 4
11 + 17	5 + 14	6 + 10

Math Made Easy....

Name : _______________________

Direction: Add the number of images in each box and
write the answer in the last box.

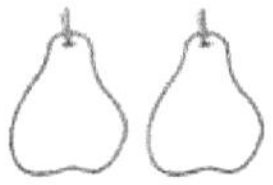

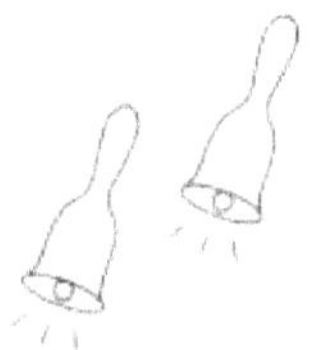

4
+ 9

Answer

1
+ 1

Answer

3
+ 10

Answer

3
+ 6

Answer

3
+ 9

Answer

5
+ 7

Answer

Addition Worksheets

2	2	10
+ 14	+ 14	+ 15

8	10	5
+ 5	+ 9	+ 20

5	5	13
+ 19	+ 11	+ 9

Name : _______________________

Direction: Add the number of images in each box and write the answer in the last box.

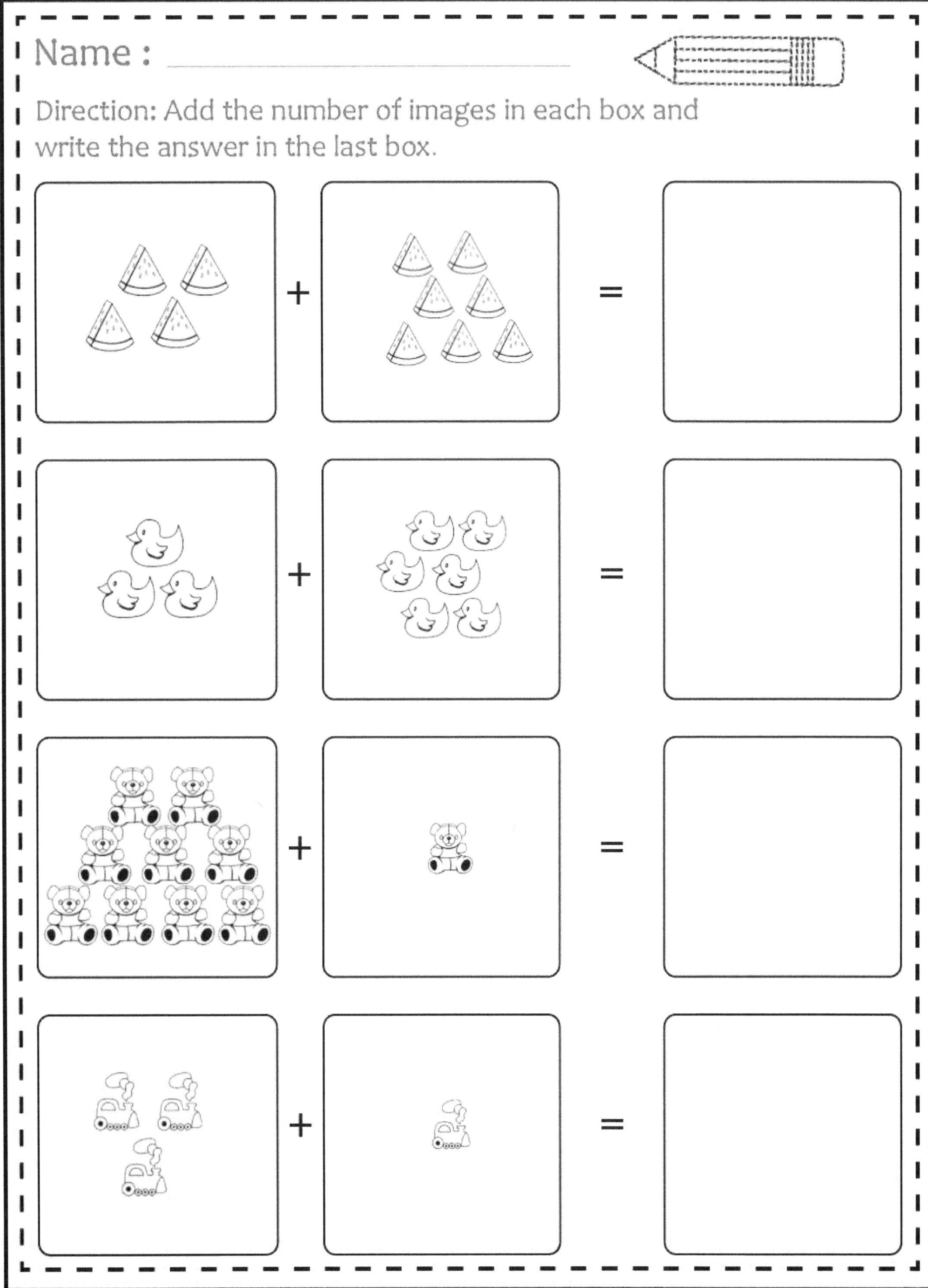

Addition Worksheets

5
+ 5

[ ] Answer

2
+ 6

[ ] Answer

1
+ 10

[ ] Answer

6
+ 5

[ ] Answer

5
+ 4

[ ] Answer

2
+ 1

[ ] Answer

Addition Worksheets

```
   6          20         14
+  6        + 14       +  5
______      ______     ______
[    ]      [    ]     [    ]


  18          11         14
+  2        +  4       + 11
______      ______     ______
[    ]      [    ]     [    ]


   5          18         17
+  4        +  1       + 14
______      ______     ______
[    ]      [    ]     [    ]
```

Name : _______________

Direction: Add the number of images in each box and write the answer in the last box.

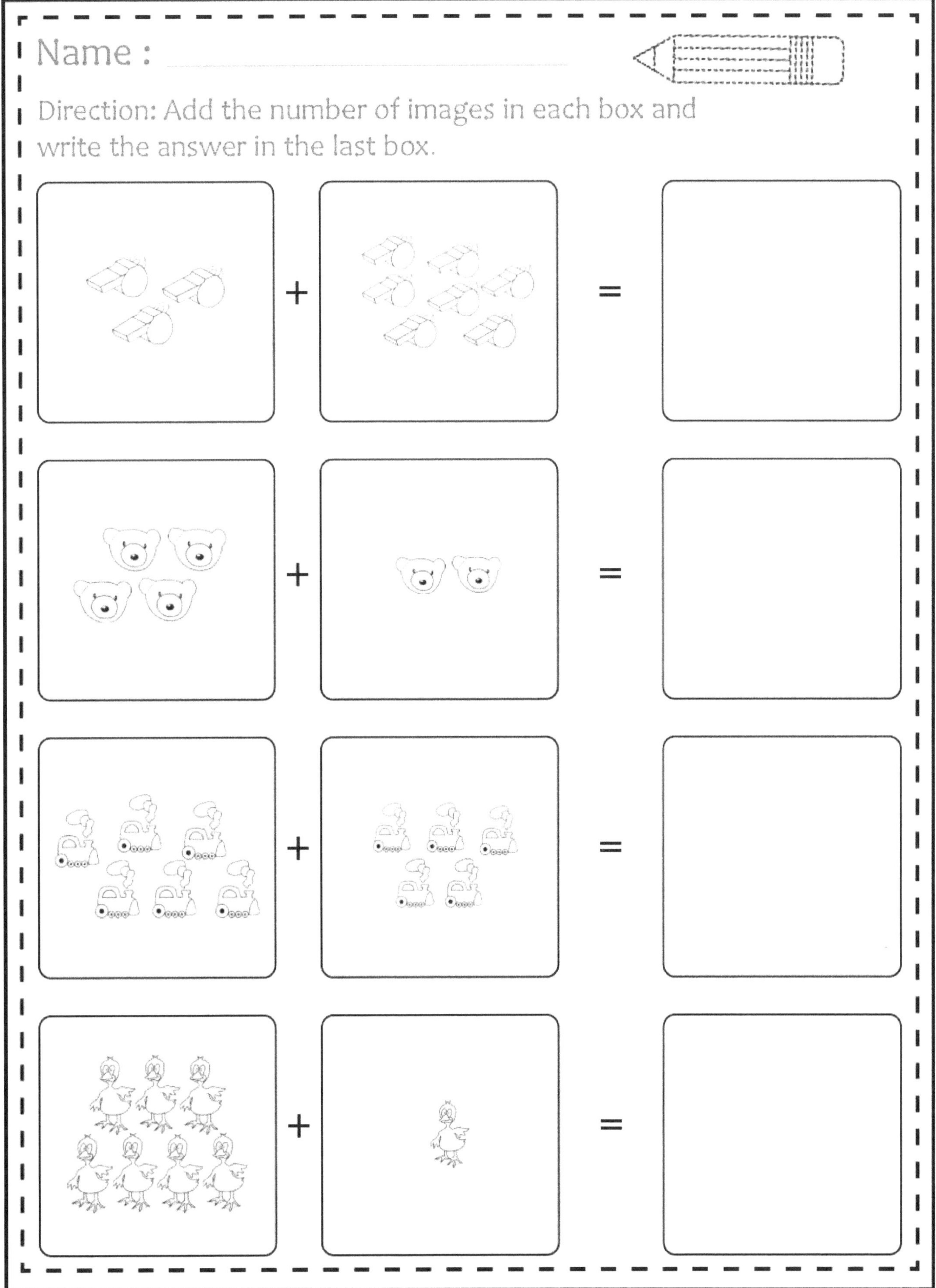

2
+ 4 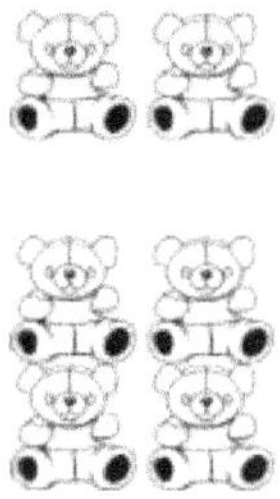
Answer

1
+ 2 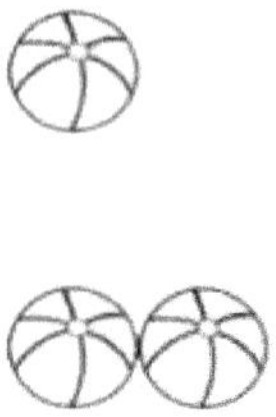
Answer

2
+ 1 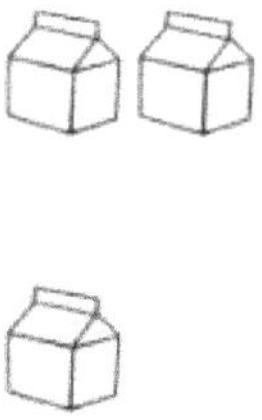
Answer

4
+ 1 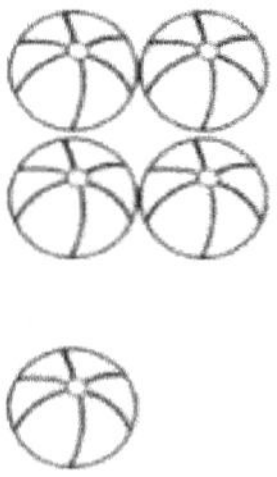
Answer

2
+ 6 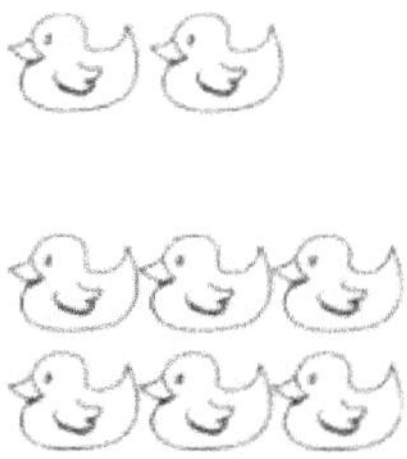
Answer

4
+ 7 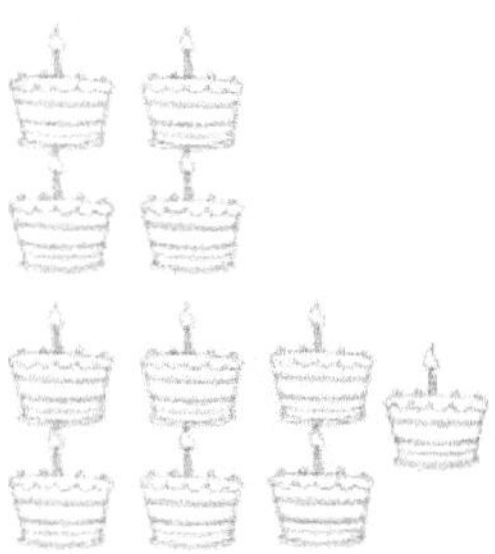
Answer

Addition Worksheets

2 + 16	16 + 8	1 + 8
15 + 11	5 + 6	13 + 19
8 + 9	9 + 16	14 + 15

Direction: Add the number of images in each box and write the answer in the last box.

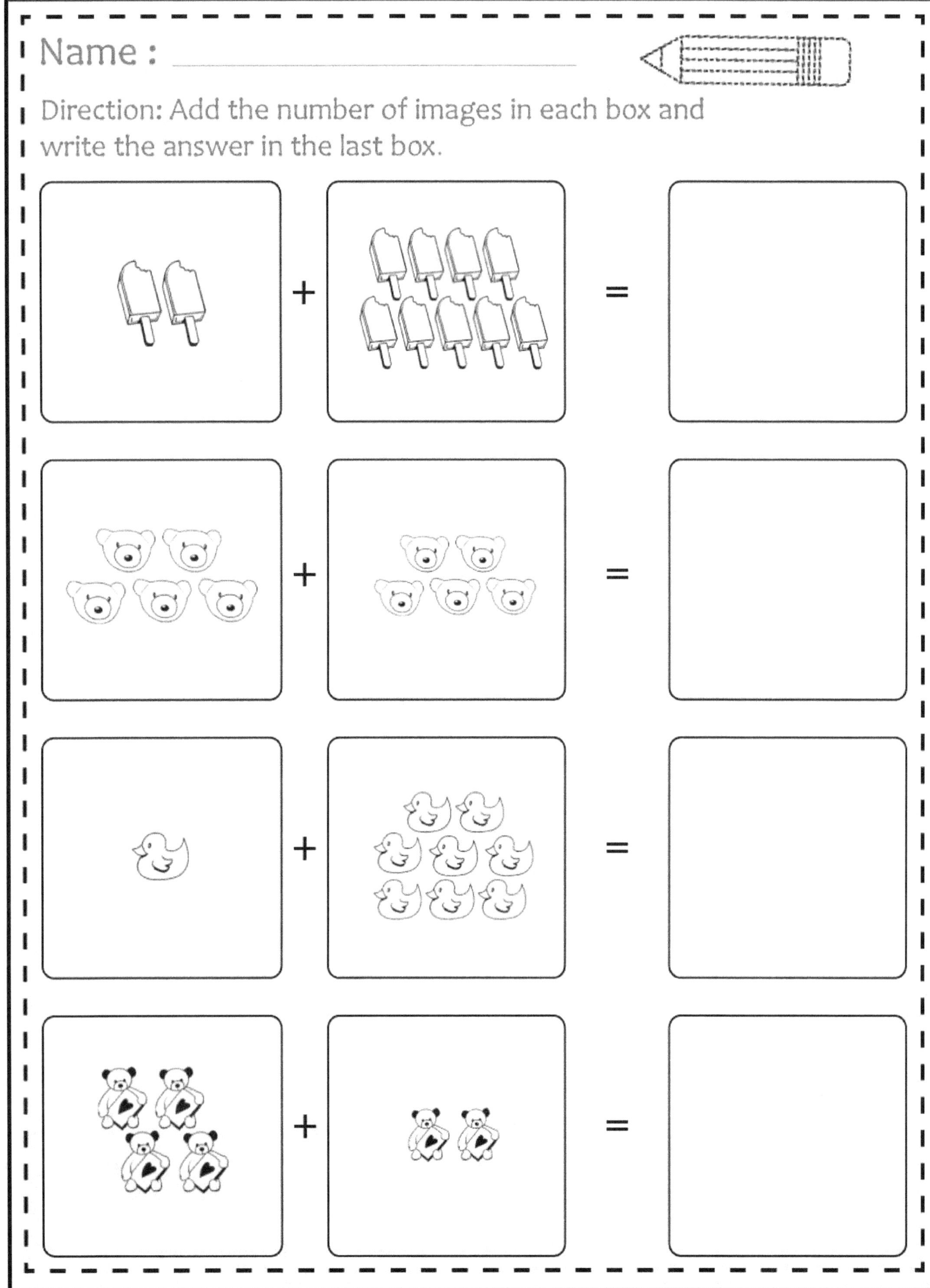

6 + 4 **Answer**	4 + 5 **Answer**
3 + 2 **Answer**	4 + 6 **Answer**
5 + 7 **Answer**	3 + 4 **Answer**

Name : ______________________

Addition Worksheets

| 9 | 13 | 4 |
| + 15 | + 4 | + 20 |

| 7 | 11 | 6 |
| + 6 | + 8 | + 19 |

| 19 | 4 | 8 |
| + 6 | + 5 | + 15 |

Math Made Easy....

Name : _______________________

Direction: Add the number of images in each box and
write the answer in the last box.

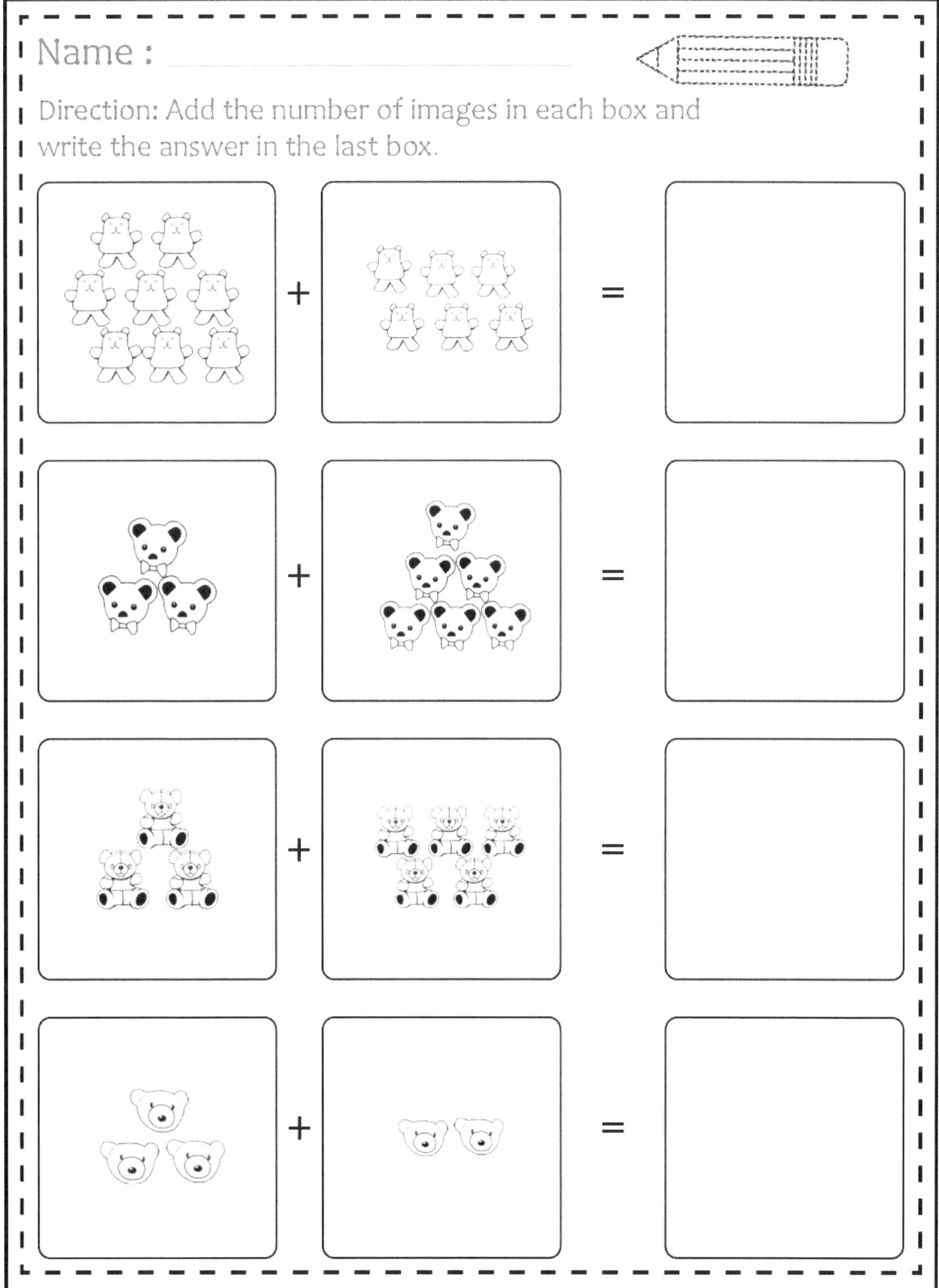

4
+ 6

Answer

5
+ 5

Answer

6
+ 5

Answer

5
+ 10

Answer

4
+ 10

Answer

6
+ 8

Answer

Name : _______________________

Addition Worksheets

14 + 16	

$$14 + 16$$

$$18 + 17$$

$$17 + 18$$

$$6 + 16$$

$$7 + 20$$

$$18 + 17$$

$$10 + 2$$

$$17 + 9$$

$$12 + 9$$

Math Made Easy....

Direction: Add the number of images in each box and
write the answer in the last box.

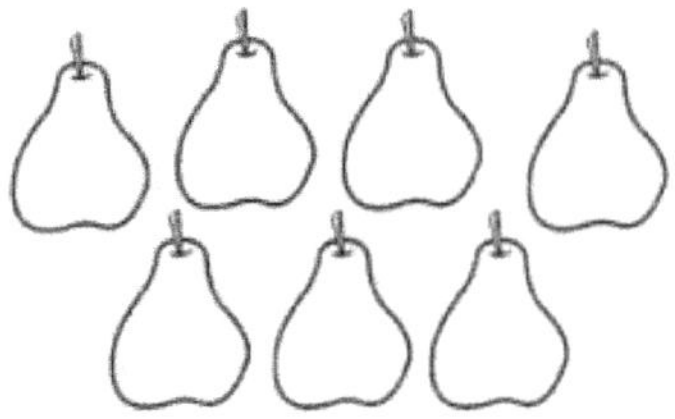

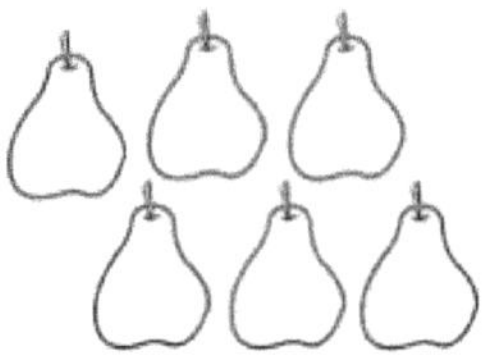

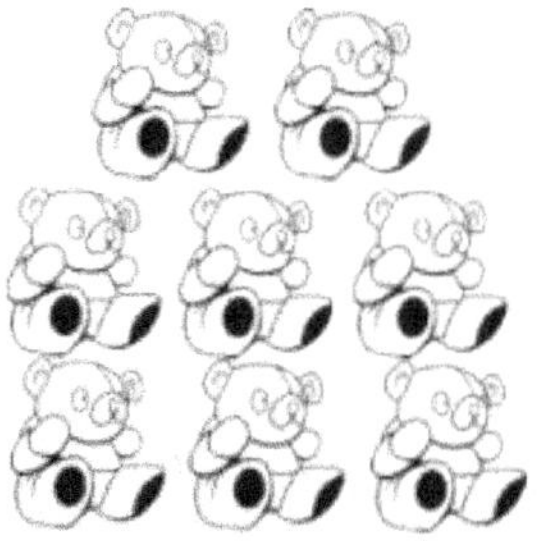

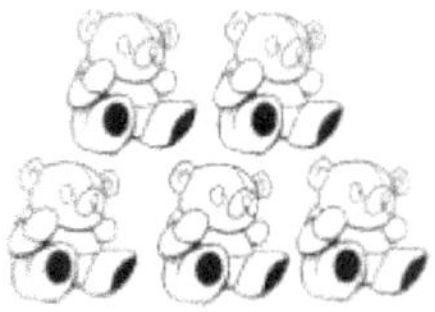

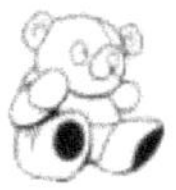

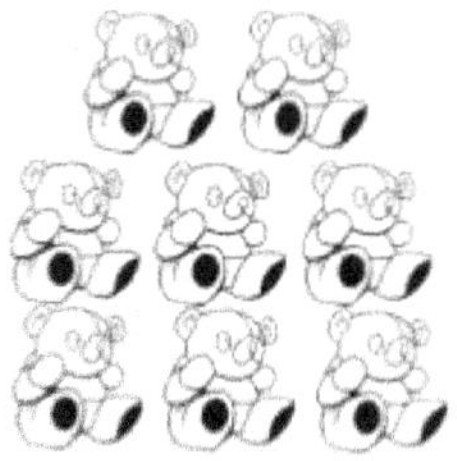

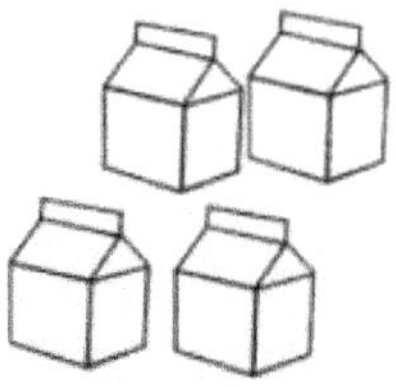

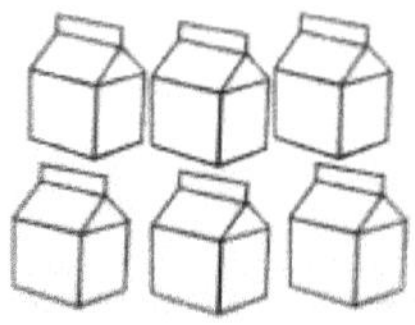

Addition Worksheets

4
+ 9

Answer

2
+ 7

Answer

3
+ 4

Answer

1
+ 6

Answer

3
+ 8

Answer

3
+ 6

Answer

Addition Worksheets

2 + 7	2 + 13	5 + 19
2 + 11	12 + 16	10 + 6
14 + 10	10 + 3	19 + 7

Name : _______________________

Direction: Add the number of images in each box and
write the answer in the last box.

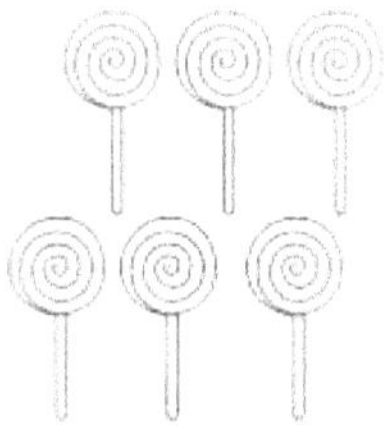

Addition Worksheets

6
+ 2

[ ] Answer

5
+ 2

[ ] Answer

6
+ 4

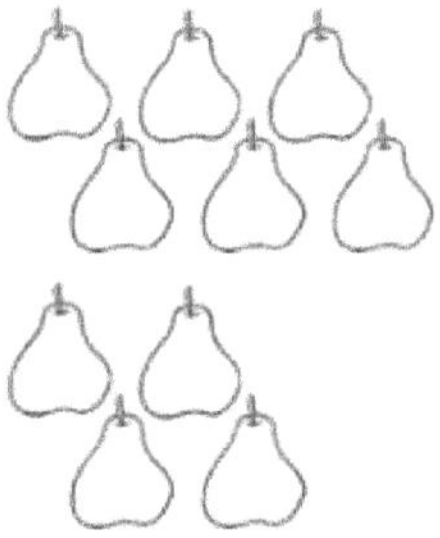

[ ] Answer

6
+ 8

[ ] Answer

6
+ 8

[ ] Answer

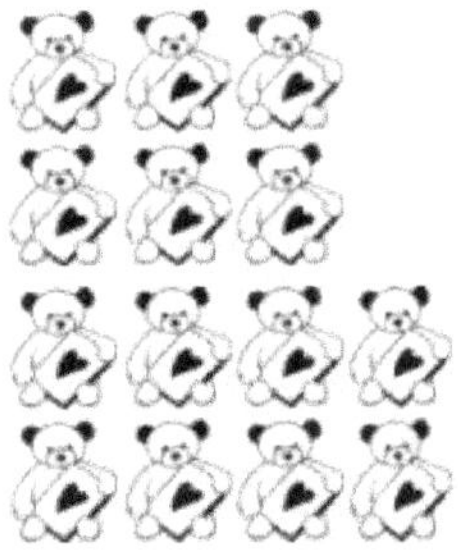

2
+ 9

[ ] Answer

Addition Worksheets

Name : ________________

Addition Worksheets

10 + 1	11 + 7	19 + 2
20 + 12	4 + 20	12 + 1
5 + 1	2 + 8	9 + 20

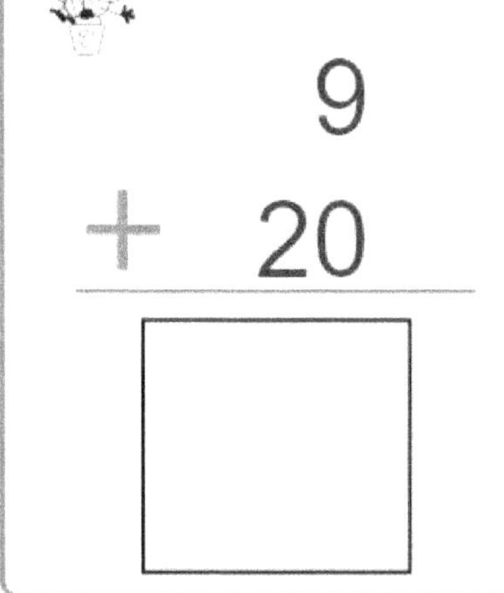

Math Made Easy....

Name : _______________________

Direction: Add the number of images in each box and write the answer in the last box.

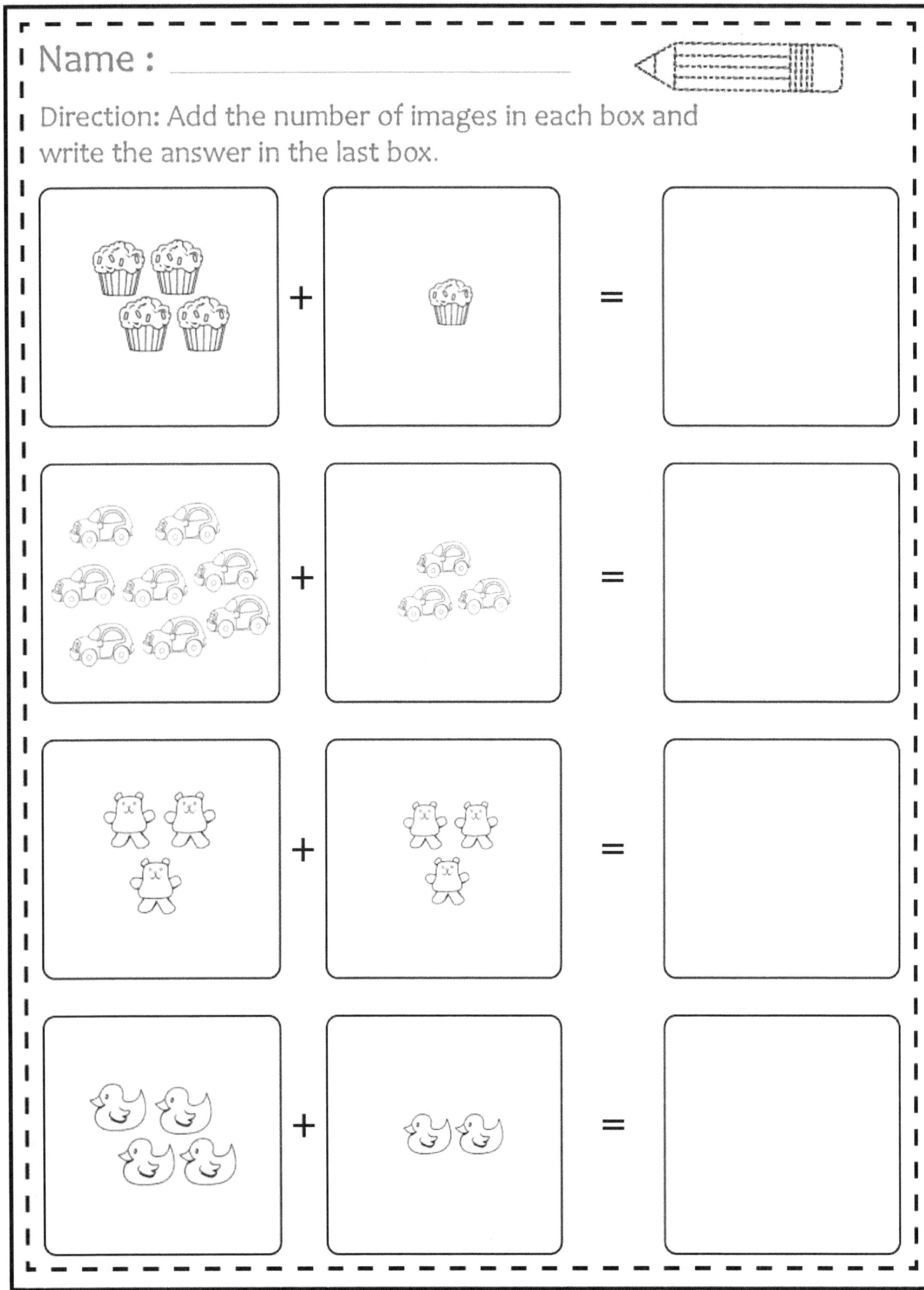

Addition Worksheets

6
+ 8

Answer

3
+ 3

Answer

2
+ 6

Answer

4
+ 7

Answer

1
+ 8

Answer

4
+ 3

Answer